UNLIMITED GOD
written by Alberta Quigley
1st Edition © 2025 by Alberta Quigley
ISBN: 979-8-218-79051-6

Scripture quotations taken from the KING JAMES VERSION (KJV):, public domain.

To book Apostle Alberta for a speaking engagement, personal prayer, or to order books by bulk contact Apostle at: (719) 478-6153

Scan the QR code to sow into Apostle Alberta Quigley's Ministry:

Support AQM

TABLE OF CONTENTS

Alberta Quigley has a deep passion for Jesus and a tender heart for people. She longs to see lives set free through the freedom she has received from God. Flowing in the gifts of the Holy Spirit, particularly the word of wisdom and knowledge, she helps others release their burdens to Jesus and walk in forgiveness. Her message on forgiveness is powerful and unique, breaking shackles off of people's lives and ushering in healing.

Her ministry is marked by signs, wonders, and miraculous healings. Alberta's life story, from brokenness to freedom, is nothing short of inspiring. This is a must-read book. It's been a true joy in my life to be part of her journey forward.

- Apostle Phil DeBord

I've had the privilege of ministering alongside Alberta over the past few years, and it's clear that she lives and breathes to serve Jesus. Her spiritual gifts—particularly in words of knowledge and inner healing—are both sharp and deeply impactful.

This book is a powerful reflection of Alberta's journey, woven with testimonies of the Lord's miraculous work in her life. At its heart lies a humble question: "Why would the Lord use someone like me?" Through this vulnerable inquiry, Alberta invites readers to see that if God can use her, He can use anyone—if only we're willing to surrender ourselves fully to Him, without conditions.

Her stories will stir your spirit, strengthen your faith, and remind you that availability to God is often the only qualification He requires.

-Dr. Chet McBroom
Executive Pastor of Hearts of Fire Church
Federal Way, Washington

Chapter 1: Divine Protection and the Call to Support Law Enforcement

I would like to share some personal experiences of engaging with police officers, their struggles and the importance of forgiveness in their profession, highlighting the protection that police officers need and the spiritual support the community can offer.

The Lord sends me around the country through the broadcast airwaves and, on my travels, to teach the body of Christ 3 key points:

1. Importance of Police Protection -

Revealing the crucial role that police officers play in maintaining societal order, referencing the dangers they face daily while putting the revelation of unlimited divine protection in its proper context.

2. Forgiveness and Healing -

Illustrating why a significant focus is on forgiveness, as illustrated through an account of police officer Ray Seabourg, who would ultimately forgive his shooter in court. I want to emphasize how deeply impactful this was to him and the emotional toll it takes on all officers, when they experience this type of emotional trauma and why this is important.

3. Why Community Engagement and Support?

I want to encourage community involvement through prayer and support for police officers, because the Lord has showed me that this initiative is crucial for mental and emotional health within the law enforcement community.

This is not just a book, it's a work-book really, designed to help you believe the Lord for an unlimited supply in every area, so that you can take your resources and the knowledge here, and give it out to those whom you minister to. On that note, I want to begin with a question, "What is it to be protected?" Well, myself and some of my ministry partners been doing meetings with the police and, I ministered exclusively for 10 years with one policeman. He's in heaven now. I held his hand as he was dying. Another one in Houston, Paul Day, he's now in heaven, too. We also did ministry together, and I learned to respect our police officers. Right now, a lot of them are hurting. We started these meetings for them. What I have found out is that forgiveness fits in with this ministry too. I want to describe that a little bit in this chapter. We had a breakfast and a policeman in Washington by the name of Ray Seabourg, He was the speaker and it was so successful that we had a prayer lunch too and he was the speaker for that as well. In Matthew 18 Peter asked Jesus, he said;

"Jesus, how often should I forgive if a man trespass against me, till seven times?"

Jesus said, no, seven times 70. You may not believe this but I know a lot of police officers, and you know what? They have to forgive almost every day. I'm going to tell you what happens to them. They see all kinds of bad stuff when they go out on the call. It's their reality. So, Ray Seabourg was a police officer there in the state of Washington and we had him come and speak. He explained what happened to him. He went on a call, got out of the car, and a man shot him twice in his legs. He fell down. Then the guy came over and was going to kill him. Ray begged him. He said, "I have a wife, and I have children. Please don't kill me." and the guy drew back the gun and decided not to shoot him in the head. The guy ran away but as he was running away, he shot the officer twice more in his body.

Ray is a very strong Christian - a very strong Christian police officer. How many of you know there is strength in Jesus! It took him a while to get even to where he could walk. It took courage to come to our meeting until a lot of people came, a lot of citizens that wanted to support the police. They came and, the last luncheon we had with him, he told us about it all, and he was crying when he said it. He said that in court he forgave the shooter. He faced the shooter and told the judge, "I forgive this young man." The man was young, about 30 years old. He forgave that shooter. How many of you, as you read this, could do that? I don't know if I could. I mean that's something else.

There was another time, that I made friends with a policeman. I was ministering to him as we were in the church parking lot. We got to know each other because he would come there to park and do his reports. He felt safe there. He said, "Yeah, my partner was shot in the head right in front of me." "Oh my goodness." I said. Beloved, do you know what in the world these men go through, and women?" Not just the men, it's the women, too. So, we've started a movement in the state of Washington - to hold these meetings and let the community know more about what their police officers do. They go through a lot of drama and trauma. I went for a ride with one and we went up to northern Washington. There are things they have to see, they can't just ignore it and turn a blind eye like all of us.

For example, a woman was speeding on the freeway. I won't name the place, but she was drunk. She had five kids in the car. She ran her car into an embankment. The baby was thrown out onto the highway and the other four kids were burned alive with their mom in the car. The police had to patrol and pick up that mess. People wonder why the police get so traumatized. There's more, we have suicides going on in the police department. That's right. They see so much and are treated so badly. In the past, they've had rocks thrown at them. They've also been defunded, they've been stabbed. They've been shot. It's time for the body of Christ to come together and pray for them. This is where the need is, and I pray you can sense the urgency in my words.

As we are talking about protection - It's right there in Psalms 91. I want to get into that, how people can start believing for God's protection. It's one thing that the police protect us. God bless the police for trying and God sets up government and people around us for protection, but it's ultimately him that protects us. So, we should start praying for our protectors, so to speak. I'm not saying we are not. Many are, but we should all be praying for them. We are the believers. We should do our best to encourage them, to pray for them. If not you, who? If not now, when? We are best to speak highly of them, to treat them decently, do something for them, help them. They have busy schedules; It's a lot of work. It's a lot of trauma and it's up to us as believers to help them understand that it's God that gets them through every shift. If we'll believe our prayers that we're praying over them, so they know they're washed over with the blood of Christ every day they go out on that job in the morning, afternoon, or night, whatever it is, no matter what circumstances, God will provide that kind of protection. Can I get an amen here?

Now - What is Psalm 91? Psalm 91:11 - The angels. God will give his angels charge over them. That is the critical scripture to really define what I'm talking about;

> *"For he shall give his angels charge over thee, to keep thee in all thy ways."*

We've got that now with our movement for the police - to love the police more. We have been using that as the main scripture for this. There are a lot of police, for example on my Facebook, that I connect with. I've got so many different states where the police officers are sending me information, and I send them back some 911's in the spirit realm and then I try to encourage the people with these requests. This has got to be what it is about with this divine protection. We cover law enforcement as the angels go to work and protect them and us all! I tell people so that they can understand this kind of protection, if your teenagers are out running the street at night guess who's watching over them. When the house is being broken into, I'm not going to call ghostbusters - I'm going call 911 and there they go. My friend Pat, she is why we started this movement. Her son was a police officer, and he was dispatched to a family feud. Law enforcement goes to a lot of those. He was trying to protect the family. A man snuck up behind him and shot him right in the head. He shot him in the head when he was trying to protect a family. Can you imagine? They go to these types of calls.

Another instance, in the state of Washington, five police officers were out just going to have coffee, enjoying themselves off duty when a gunman comes in and shoots them. As a minister to the boys and girls in blue, I want to encourage the body of Christ that they can have regular meetings in their churches to pray for our police because, could you imagine what it would be like without them? I believe in the book of John - that God created everything. I believe God created law enforcement. Why? To protect his people. What if we didn't have them? That's right, It would be complete chaos. So, for Ray to get up there and say, "I forgave.", is powerful. For him to lay there and have to plead for his life should be a wakeup call to all of us about the importance of their work. Another one in the state of Washington occurred when an officer was on the side of the road making out a report and a drunken driver came and hit him head on. I'm writing this to ask you to please begin praying for our police for their protection?

We've started this movement and it's going to go all over the United States. I also work with a man by the name of Daryl Russell. He was in law enforcement for 25 years. He still does things with law enforcement, but we get together and we get the citizens involved and we want them to know, especially the Christians. But where are they? Why aren't they praying? Do the police get angry? Probably and especially when they see kids abused and when they go to a family feud. I've seen it firsthand.

This is my to appeal to the body of Christ to consider the ones who live Psalms 91, on all of our be halves. They don't do it for themselves; they do it for us. Please lift them up in prayer. Consider to get a prayer meeting going in your church or on a phone call for them. If you have any idea what they go through - they want to come home safely to their families. Prayer is the key. That's what I am asking - is that you raise them up with a covering of prayer and then claim Psalm 91:11, not only for them, but yourself and your family. Psalms 91 is an unlimited chapter. Let's use it and believe God.

Chapter 2: Humility in Ministry

I believe what I'm going to say here will truly bless you. I want to go low and talk about some of my hardships and difficulties in my walk with the Lord, to be real and let you know I am not perfect either but how the Lord, in his goodness, will meet us where we are at and make the crooked road straight, especially in our hearts, because the path from your heart to your head is sometimes sabotaged by the enemy. The battle truly is in the mind saints. As you read on, you're going to see how the Lord will intervene and allow for the 5 R's to begin working – renewal, restoration, repair, resolution and revival to bring you to a place of true servanthood. Come on somebody.

I remember a trip to Tennessee where I was invited to take part in, at the time, a popular national Christian TV production. I actually remember it like it was yesterday, there were financial constraints, and this trip would serve to be a strong lesson about humility and reliance on God's provision. I would come to learn the importance of being grounded and how important being humble really is in ministry. Now, contrary to what I thought would happen on this trip, I would find myself being assigned minor roles and was faced with having to dig deep and find humility in my interactions with other actors who were a part of this production. I want to highlight some of those moments of personal revelation, where I came to discover unlimited forgiveness the way Jesus displayed it. I would go on to learn about the necessity of forgiveness, which ultimately led to a successful performance that year in Tennessee.

I just know that this will be a source of encouragement to you reader, about God's guidance and favor in your ministry which is why, in the course of writing this book and in the preparations leading up to it I often have asked myself, "Why would God use a woman like me?" You know, he uses the foolish things of the world to confound the wise. Especially the foolishness of how we sometimes think we are being humble, when we really are not. This book is the perfect reason to reflect these thoughts off of you, to inspire us all to truly come to know that our God is unlimited in every way. That we can understand and walk into the promises that he has for all of us.

So, I ask you, Have you ever been played? Have you ever been haughty or high minded or found yourself in a situation where you had to be truly humble and allow God to restore you to a right standing so that you can be used of Him. Don't answer that. I know the answer, of course you have! You and I need the grace and forgiveness of God everyday in order to be used of Him. Fortunately for you and me, He has an unlimited supply. You might be saying, "What is that, Alberta? How do you mean?" Well as I said, about 10 or 15 years ago, I was invited to go to this Tennessee TV studio to do a play. Most of us ministers in Washington cut our teeth on this Christian TV Network. This particular time they called me up and said, "Alberta, you want to come and be in a play in Hendersonville?" I said yes and I immediately went to my church. But the problem was, I didn't have any money to travel to Tennessee from Washington state.

My pastor said, "We're going to take up a collection and we're going to pay your way there." So, they collected $415 in total and the Lord, in his own unlimited way, made a way where there was no way. I was so happy to see this. The Lord wasn't finished, a lawyer friend of mine from Houston called and she said, "Hey Alberta, we hear you're going down there to Hendersonville." I said, "Yes I am." She responded, "I am hiring a woman to drive you over there, so when you get off the plane, you're going to have this woman all dressed up, you know, and she's taking you to Hendersonville." "Oh, wow", I thought, "Boy, I finally arrived. Now I get a limousine to go in." How many of you know that Romans 8:28 says;

> *"All things work together for the good to them that love the Lord and are called according to his purpose."*

But I had the attitude of, "I've been on TV so many times. Boy, they're going to roll out the red carpet for me. I finally arrived." Then that lawyer got me way down to Hendersonville and I had my driver in a nice blue suit and everything with the big sign that said 'Alberta Quigley' at my arrival to the airport. I thought, "I'm finally getting somewhere!" How many of you know pride goes before a fall?

So, we got to Hendersonville. Now, I forgot to ask where I was going to stay. Well, truth is I didn't know that the leadership at that TV station was very discerning. They knew that if I was going to come there, then I would provide my own lodging. In this way, it would prove to them that I really wanted to be there. So, I drove up to the office and I sent the chauffeur in, and I said, "Tell them I'm here." She came back and she said, "They said that you have to find your own place to stay." I said, "Oh!" In my holiness, I really was surprised at that. She said, "Well, where am I going to drop you off at?" I happened to see a little outdoor cafe near there. I said, "Take me over there." I got out of that, limousine and I wondered, even was somewhat bewildered. I sat down on a bench because I didn't know where I was going to go, where I was going to stay. But how many of you know God makes the plans? I need an amen right here so you can catch this next part as you read on.

We need, we just simply need to follow and walk in Him. So, I sat down on the bench, and I said to God, "You know what, Lord, I really missed it. You know, I know where you guide, you provide. You paid for the airline ticket." After I tipped the chauffeur, I only had a few dollars left. I said again, "Lord, I missed it. Now what am I going to do?" Pretty soon this van drives up and says, "Hey." It turned out to be the dressmaker, the one who did all the costumes for the production I flew there to be a part of. She said, "Hey, anybody need a place to stay?" "I do!", I exclaimed. She replied, "Well,

I'll tell you, you're going with me, but at the end, you have to pay for the room and help pay for this place. I said, "Okay." There again, I didn't have any money, but I said, okay anyway. My faith was up but inside I felt a little entitled, that I was in demand and sought after for my ministry and that someone should pay my expenses.

Right there, the Lord was already at work intervening. I stayed there and the next day, at our arrival to the studio they instructed us that they were going to pick the roles for everybody in the play. Now, we go up there on the stage and the director says, "Okay, Alberta, you're going to be Lazarus' mother." I immediately replied, "I don't want to be his mother. I want to be his sister." Pride, you know. He said, "No, you're going to be the mother." I said again, this time with more intent, "I don't really want to be the mother." He said, "You're going to be the mother." He was resolute in his voice. "Oh, my goodness! Okay." I uttered. Then he said, "By the way, you're going to be a policeman" He rattled off a few more roles he had me down for. I said, "Okay.", even though I was not ok with it. The dressmaker then came to me. I was saying, okay, but getting that attitude. The dressmaker says, "Alberta, we're going over to the second-hand store to buy your costumes." I said, "You what?" I was mortified. "We've got to go to the second-hand store." she replied. I said with a cynical tone, "Oh, okay. You know, I like going there anyway." In my mind I thought, "What is this? I've got to go buy my costume?"

So, we go into the second-hand store, and I find a little hat. Well, it turns out Betty Jean Robinson, she was going to be Jesus' mother and I got stuck with being Lazarus' mother. So I bought this old hat, and I thought, "What am I buying this for?" This whole situation had me feeling as sour as old grapes. I didn't know, but this old hat would turn out to be for Betty Jean Robinson. She took a look at it and said, "I want that hat." I said to her, "I don't know why I bought it." as I gave it to her. I also had to buy a make-believe gun to be the police officer too. I would come to have five different parts in that production. I'm not boasting on that at all. Any of you ministers out there, if you think you got it, if you think like I did: "Oh, you know, I finally made it. Oh, yes and I get to be in this play that reaches throughout the world. Well, I got it made.", you have the wrong attitude. There is no humility in that. You talk about pride. I didn't like me after what I was beginning to see. See, God wanted me to go to that second-hand store to get that hat and get me some costumes. I knew then, the Lord was saying, "If you're going to come here, then you're coming for one reason, and that is to serve me."

I was also meant to stay in that apartment because they had a lot of ministry going on in there. The truth is I needed to be ministered to, and I know this story is sure to change your perspective on walking in humility because it changed mine. So, we arrive for rehearsal and they say, "Okay, Alberta, let's go rehearse." All of us were there and the director says, "Now Alberta, when Lazarus comes out, we want you all to cry." Well, the truth was we couldn't cry. The director then said, "Why can't these people cry? The co-founder of the TV network then ran up on the stage. She was a highly anointed and mighty woman of God. She said, "You know why they can't cry.... they have no anointing." She immediately came and laid hands on every one of us. Suddenly, we all cried! What a humbling experience that was. Restoration and renewal of our hearts was beginning to take place. So finally, here comes Lazarus out of the tomb and we're all crying. The actor playing Lazarus then comes up to me and he says, "I hear you do deliverance prayers." I replied, "Yeah, I do." "Well, after the show, I want you to do deliverance on me." he exclaimed. He continued," I'm not right with God right now." I replied, "You aren't?" He said, "No." I said, "And you're Lazarus?" with a hint of sarcasm in my tone. "Well, get the authority from the leaders here and I'll pray for you." I said reluctantly.

How many know, if you're going to pray for somebody, get permission before you do? Don't just jump in, get an agreement with those in authority over the meeting. Well, I did get permission and we got underneath the stage and Lazarus, I'll tell you, we got to praying and he fell to the ground and got totally set free. It was powerful. I thought, "Boy, he came out of the tomb, and now he's set free." But my attitude still wasn't good. How many of you know that God makes plans? Yes. He makes plans for us that we know not of. The Lord was setting me up to really learn.

The directors then come and get me, and they say, "Alberta, look at this big rock. It goes up high and Jesus is going to be on the top of this rock, and we want you to sit right here in front of the rock, right on the stones, so the whole world can see you." Oh boy, this was great. Now the whole world will see me. I'm serious when I tell you that, unfortunately, that was my attitude then. I cannot be clearer than to say to you, don't you all be boasting about what you've been on and where you've been and all that.

So, I was sitting on my rock and this lady who wanted to be an actor, she comes and sits down by me, and she says to me, "Get off my rock." She says it again, "Get off my rock!" I said, "This isn't your rock. This is my rock. See, it's my rock." I'm laughing now as I write this because it's funny, but it wasn't then. Just then this little 12-year-old girl comes up and she says, "Can I sit on the rock?" We both looked at each other and I say, "Let's give the rock to her. Let's sit on the floor." The actor says to me, "By the way, I hear you pray for people. Will you come back by the costume room and lay hands on me?" I thought, "I'll lay hands on you alright." See, my ego and pride were wounded because she seemingly wanted to take my position in the play and prevent me from being seen. How many know Alberta had a bad attitude that day? I'm telling you, ministry can go sideways when you get too high-minded.

From the get-go, I had stinking thinking. My heart rationalized in my mind, "I've been on TV so many times and surely when I pull up, it's going to be red carpet treatment." I was arriving there to be served, forgetting that the very reason I was called there was to serve in the very powerful channels of media ministry. Well, the producers were very wise. The one in charge was a well-known woman of God and she let everybody come, but she made sure that we were all coming for the right reason. She was no stranger to what a big platform and bright lights could do to quench the Holy Spirit. After that encounter at the rock and after I prayed for this actor and she got set free, we then grew to love each other. Listen, Revelation 3:7-8 declares;

"7 And to the angel of the church in Philadelphia write; These things saith he that is holy, he that is true, he that hath the key of David, he that openeth, and no man shutteth; and shutteth, and no man openeth; 8 I know thy works: behold, I have set before thee an open door, and no man can shut it: for thou hast a little strength, and hast kept my word, and hast not denied my name."

The Lord shuts the door and it's shut. Lord God, I would ask you that everyone looking at these pages, let them know that where you guide, you provide. There are some ministers reading and you are absolutely afraid to go anywhere without a dime in your pocket. Well, I can tell you stories where (and I will in my forthcoming books) I have been where I haven't had a dime in my pocket, but God called me there. See, that's the difference. HE calls you there. Come on, agree with me;

*Father, in the name of Jesus Christ, I ask you to
provide for every minister, every ministry, and
those people being trained for ministry. If you're
a Christian, you do have a ministry and so I pray,
Lord, provide for everyone. Help us, Lord God, not
to get big-headed. Yes, but help us to give you all the
praise, all the glory, and every ounce of honor for
every door you open. We can't take any of the glory
and honor. Amen.*

Chapter 3: Provision from the Unlimited God

I want to now focus on the intersection of faith and finances, to emphasize the unlimited provision of God and the importance of obedience to divine guidance. I want to use money as the theme to show that everyone needs money and should not limit God's ability to provide because in His unlimited resource and wisdom, He will provide. I also want to encourage you to believe that pursuing God results in rewards.

Within these pages are, as you have seen so far, personal anecdotes detailing miraculous provisions in my life, my early ministry struggles, there was even an empty fridge while caring for my grandson. I know you will really enjoy that one. God's unlimited provision was shown to me through these personal experiences, including being instructed to wait by a river only to find money there, which taught me to demonstrate faith and obedience to the voice of the Lord.

God's provision isn't just a momentary miracle but part of a lesson in trusting Him. I discovered that there is a connection between faith, obedience, and miraculous acts. I've also seen that the need for continuous guidance is real but, learned how God understands that and that he reveals necessary provisions, especially in our desperate hour. Here we go, we're going to talk about your favorite subject, money. Who doesn't need money? This chapter is sure to take the chains, the handcuffs, the restraints off of your finances - taking God out of the box to be the unlimited God that he is. Why should we limit him to anything when he's unlimited to do anything?

When I first started the ministry, I took care of my little grandson, he was about four or five at the time. I was taking care of him, and we had no money to eat, and it was the weekend, and I said, "Lord, the fridge is empty. Uh, I have no money to eat, what am I going to do, Lord? I have this little boy here." You know what he told me? "Go down and wait in Cedar River....and you'll find the money." I was penniless at that point. You might be thinking, "Well, how did you get in that shape?" I don't even remember how I got there, but I was there. Now, I was young in the ministry, and I thought, "Boy, now this is talking about provision because at that moment I remembered Philippians 4:19:

"For my God shall supply all my needs according to his riches in glory by and through Christ Jesus our only Lord and Savior."

According to his riches in glory - I mean, His heaven is so vast and look at his creation and the telescope which man can use to peer into His glory. He's letting man get in on all of his creation. I can tell you this, God can cause you to prosper. I've seen it so many times in my life.

So, I grabbed my little grandson, and I said, "Okay Lord, I'll do that." The river wasn't deep. Do you know we got in that river, and I found a lot of money in that river? Can I get an amen! I didn't know people threw quarters in the river, but God knows, they do it for love. So, as I said, we went down there and we found plenty of money - my little grandson and I together. Well, you might be saying, "Alberta, why didn't God just send somebody to your house with the provision you needed? Well, I needed to learn that - I needed to learn that lesson. See, you know that I was just starting out in ministry, and I couldn't believe that there was money in that river. the Lord provided miraculously. That was the lesson.

Then another thing happened as I drove down to speak at a meeting. The pastor gave me a check, a love gift, after the meeting but here's another lesson I had to learn. I didn't fill up my gas tank and I didn't have one penny before this meeting. So, I drove away from that church with only a check at 10:00 at night and I pulled over to the gas station and I said, "Lord, how am I going to get home? I'm past empty. I'll run out on the way home." This is powerful, I had about 10 or 15 miles to go, maybe more, until I arrived home. I thought, "How am I going to get home?" You know what the Lord told me? - "Look in your car." I did and I found money under the seats, I found money in the glove box, I found all kinds of money in that car that I didn't even know I had. I found enough money to put the gas in the car to make it home.

So, a few days later the Pastor called me, and he happened to be blessed with a lot of money. He has a very powerful ministry. He said, "Alberta, I am at the restaurant. You know, I forgot my cards and all that stuff at home. Will you pray for me right now? I can't leave this restaurant without paying." I said, "Listen Pastor, go out and look in your car. You'll find enough money to pay that bill." He went out and looked in his car. Sure enough he did, and he was able to cover that meal. He said, "Alberta, I didn't know I had so much in that car."

Even recently as I write this in summer of 2025, I was invited to tape my television program live in Southern California with a Christian TV network. I had to go to the Lord for the provision to go. I said, "Lord, where you guide you do provide. Please provide so I can go there to do my programs and so I can go over to Colorado Springs after my broadcasting." Do you know what? God spoke to one lady, a friend of mine, that I have known for years. She sent me $1,000 and of course, I paid the tithes out of it. That paid for the programming also but here's the thing, the kicker, where the Lord really showed me how he absolutely honors our faith in Him, somebody else called and said, "Alberta, I'm sending you $500." Then another one blessed me with $100. I didn't even ask them, but I did ask God.

I want to speak into you and declare Jeremiah 33:3 over you;

"Call upon him. He'll show you great mighty things."

I was limiting God until that, I'll be honest. When that businessman put that $100 in my hand when I prayed over him and he then prayed for me I realized something. The Lord sent that man to show me, "Hey, Alberta, stop limiting me." Well, on that trip I didn't limit him. Why? Because I learned that powerful lesson through this businessman. When God said, "Alberta, if I can send that man to you like I did, and he gives you $100 without even knowing you, it is because I told him to give it! He's one of my men. Then you know what, why can't I give you whatever YOU need?" That is what the Lord said to me, and I repented right then and there. That really built my faith. I thought, "Well, yes that's true. Lord, you just had a perfect stranger do that and I didn't look poor or needy when he did it either." The Lord told him, "Put that in her hand." I'm not limiting God anymore.

Dear reader, remember the reward David was talking about. You know, that was just the natural reward. God had something spiritually more in line - King of all Israel. Can you imagine that! That was his reward for being faithful. Was he perfect? No, but that's what I'm talking about. It only works when you start claiming and sending things. The Lord has to tell you to do these things. You got to get in his word to know who he is, what he is doing, and how to be like him because he wants us all to be like him so we can have the desires of our heart to be like him and to be stress-free. We cannot go past our joy and peace. There is a promotion in the spirit when you don't limit our unlimited God.

So, don't limit the Lord. I experienced Jeremiah 33:3, I called upon God. I didn't ask this person, then God told them to send something and that was answering my prayer. I called HIM and he called them, and they heard his voice. So just call out to HIM. Yes. Then trust him to do it, even if it's a little thing like me waiting in that river with my little grandson. A lot of money was in that river. God knew it, but he was teaching me. Many times people commit suicide because they've lost their fortune. They lost everything but God can build it up again. I want to impart to you at the close of this chapter with a prayer to help you to call upon the Lord and have an expectancy to see what He wants to show you, agree with me;

So, Father, in the name of Jesus, where you guide, you do provide. Lord, I pray for provision for everyone out there that you will get the provision that's needed. I thank you, Lord, for those who have waited so long for a breakthrough. They need their house saved - their house is going into foreclosure. Lord give them I pray, in Jesus' name, what they need. I repent for all of my sins, and I forgive myself and others. I believe Lord, that you are faithful in all things. You own the cattle on a thousand hills and the hills the cattle are on. You are our creator and you are welcome to create something out of the nothings in our lives and circumstances because we are children of the King and like Ezekiel spoke to those dry bones in Ezekiel 37, we speak to those dry bank

*accounts in Jesus' name. We speak to them and say,
"You dry bank accounts, come alive in Jesus' name."
Amen.*

Chapter 4: Healing Without Limits

In this chapter, my conversation is going to center on faith, healing, and the importance of allowing God's unlimited power to work in your life. Throughout this book I have integrated spiritual teachings and personal testimonies to unpack the 'unlimited' that we receive from God as believers - not just a measure but an unlimited supply. Here I want to touch on the unlimited healing power of God by breaking down faith in God's healing power and I will emphasize the necessity of faith when facing health challenges, experienced firsthand through my testimony of healing from cancer. I want to recount my struggle with cancer following a sudden collapse at the airport, and the grim prognosis that I would not live much longer.

My hope is that, as we reflect on my experience, you can gain the understanding of how believers should not under-estimate God's ability to heal and transform lives and I want to explain the importance of having a support system, including in my experience, friends, family, and faith leaders, during my ordeal. As you will see this all led to a miraculous healing confirmation after a heart test showed a serious condition, and a later test revealed my heart as 'perfect,' showcasing God's miraculous healing.

It started when I was on a ministry trip in Wisconsin. I stopped in Minneapolis to change planes and collapsed at the airport. They had to call 911 to get me. I went to a hospital, and I'll never forget it - this old doctor sat on the foot of my bed. He said, "You have cancer." "Oh, my goodness.", I thought, and he said, more or less right out in the open, "You're not going to be here much longer. Go home. Get things in order." I thought, "Wow, cancer." He said, "As a matter of fact, don't go home. We're going to send a letter. You go right to the hospital." Wow, that was scary. I could tell how bad he felt about telling me that, more or less, "Hey, you're going to die. Get ready."

So, I flew home but before I did, I called my friend Paty and I said, "Paty, this is what I've been told." She said, "Well, Alberta, I'm going to meet you at the plane. I'm going to take you to see my doctor, Dr. Victor Oberg in Federal Way, Washington." He was a women's doctor. She said, "I'm going to give my appointment up and I'm going to take you to the hospital. I'm taking you to see Dr. Oberg." I'm writing this to show you that I learned an important lesson in not limiting God. Don't limit Him for your healing. He can do everything.

So, I go to Dr. Victor Oberg. He brings me in his office. I'd already turned yellow, by the way, and he brought me into his office. He flips around. There's this bookcase behind his desk where he whips out the Bible. He said, "Alberta, God, Jesus told me to take care of you. He told me to take care of you." Now listen, in anything I say here, I'm not boasting on me. He can do it for you. Because we can only give God all the praise and glory and honor. Don't ever try to give it to anybody else. God does the healing, and I can only give Him the glory, honor, and praise. Was I a perfect little saint, even though I had been ministering for days? No. He did it because He loved me and He wanted me healed.

So, Dr. Oberg brought his nurse in, and he said to his nurse, "Bring me some anointing oil." and they anointed me right then and there and prayed over me. You know what happened? He said, "Okay, Alberta, you're going to have to go to a cancer doctor now. I've got to send you to one." What was happening was he believed. Amen. He didn't doubt that I was going to be healed. So, I went to a cancer doctor, he was a Jewish man, and I went in and, of course, Dr. Oberg had done an examination on me. Then this cancer doctor, a very wonderful Jewish man came back, and he said, "I did the test. Yeah, it's bad. You know, and you're going to have to go in for some more tests," You know, God didn't allow me to have any pain. I had no pain. I was yellow, but I had no pain. Wow.

Dr. Oberg, he kept praying, "Well, I don't care what anybody says, you're going to be healed, you know, and that's it." How many of you know that declarations of life are so important from the people we love and care about. That's true and he would not let go of that. How many of you know that words do count? Dr. Oberg said, "Even though you're supposed to die, I'm going to believe for you." Now after my healing he said, I could use his name. He said, "Yeah, use me as a testimony because it's true. We have records, whatever we need." Anyway, the Jewish doctor said, "Okay, Alberta, what we're going to have to do is go in, send you into the hospital, and we're going to open you up and otherwise, Alberta, you might be going to heaven." Dr. Oberg still shook his head, "Alberta, no. I'm going to believe."

Dr. Oberg said, "You have to go to the hospital in Alberta and get a heart test." So we went to St. Joseph, I got a heart test, and they came out and they said, "Alberta, do you know you have a real terrible heart? Your heart is really bad." "Oh, wow." I said, "It is?" They said, "Yeah, it's bad." So, I looked at Paty and Paty looked at me and we grabbed the report. The next morning, we were supposed to go to the hospital so they could open me up and do whatever they needed to do but before that I called my pastor, Jack Bernard, and I said, "Jack, I want to do a three-day meeting. " So, he said, "Yeah, Alberta, you can have a three-day meeting."

We ended up having the meeting of all meetings. I told nobody at the church I had cancer. I kept perfectly quiet, not even my pastor knew. We danced around it, you know. I told my pastor, "I may be out of here." but I didn't give him all the details. I just said, "There's something coming up." and he said, "Go ahead." So, we danced, we shouted, we did all kinds of stuff. We were praising the Lord.

So, the next morning we went to the best hospital. He said, "Alberta, I want to put you in the best hospital here." So, he put me down in Seattle and, I'm getting ready to go in there for surgery and they said, "Where's your heart test?" I looked at Paty. I said, "Oh, we forgot it at her apartment." "Oh, that's okay. We're going to give you one." they said. I said, "Oh, no." and I looked at Paty. So, they took me in to give me the heart test and shortly after they came back out and they said, "Do you know you have a perfect heart?" I went, "What?" Now I have proof of all this. "Do you know you have a good heart?" they said, "We didn't expect you to have a heart like that." Right then I remembered that Dr. Oberg was outside praying. Then they said, "Okay, now you can get on the gurney. We're going to take you in for surgery." They were going to open me up to remove the cancer that was still there. I got it, my heart was healed.

God gave me a new heart. Now, that's been roughly about 15 years ago and my heart is still really good. I've had it examined by many people. The Lord decided He was going to create in me a new heart. Why did He do that? Is He a respecter of persons? No. He did it because Jesus Christ wanted to do it. Dr. Oberg was praying even more than his nurse. He believed even more than I did and of course the wonderful cancer doctor, he was shaking his head. I was pretty bad. Other people told me that I was out of here, but he didn't want to tell me that.

Before I went in for surgery I had told the Lord, I said, "Lord, if I make it through this surgery, I've seen their menu, and I'd like to stay here at least a week to rest. If I make it through, if I live, I want to be in this hospital so I can rest for a week, and then I can go back out again." Do you know what? They took me in for surgery. Now, this is God's truth, they opened me up and NO cancer! It was all gone. I was as clean as a whistle. I had no infections, nothing. No pain. I can prove this. I have written proof. It's funny because I expected I could order a steak dinner. Yeah right. Did you know, they came in two days later and they said, "Alberta, we need your bed. You're out of here. You're healed. You don't have anything wrong." No bad heart, no cancer, nothing. Amen.

They also said, "By the way, my friend said there's a guy, he needs prayer the next room over. Will you pray?" I said, "Sure." Here's what I want to tell you. You cannot limit God. See, I was not praying as much as my doctor was. I didn't tell my church at all except I told my pastor that I wanted to minister before I croaked but God healed me totally. When I got home, I had a meeting and he said, "Alberta, where have you been? You're lit up. My God, you have like a lighting all around you."

Then I gave my testimony and, of course, we continued the meeting. They said, "You're a new person. You look like you've lost age or what in the world?" I said, "Well," and I gave my testimony. Listen, God, what He did for me, He can do for you. Amen. He can do it. Will you let Him? Don't limit God on healing.

Chapter 5: Everlasting Life

I want to talk about someone near and dear to my heart. There is a book called <u>Arise and Shine</u> by Gloria Gillespie. I was just recently in Texas, and she had a church in Texas. She still does, although I think Pastor Troy Brewer now has that church. She's building some things for kids and everything. What a great pastor she is. I often meditate on her story found in her book, especially when the enemy tries to hit me with low blows. The testimonies in her life really have helped me to overcome my own feelings of doubt about my ministry.

I hope I can be real with you because what I'm going to share, I found, has really reminded me of the biblical perspective on life, death, and the afterlife and that this is what really matters, not the temporal world we are in today with the enemy running around trying to discourage the believer. The Bible teaches that life on earth is temporary, like a vapor. The soul, however, is eternal, and individuals face a choice between everlasting life with God or eternal destruction. Accepting Jesus Christ is the way to secure eternal life. I know most of my readers might already know that but you will find a greater perspective on that through the testimony of Gloria Gillespie writing that she witnessed Jesus personally come to her granddaughter's bedside and carry her to heaven after the child tragically drowned in a pool.

Well, one day I had gotten into a pity party. You ever get one of those? Oh, yeah, that's pretty easy to get in. I said, "Lord, you know um, I've been attacked, you know, by the people." I found myself reminding Him as if he forgot or didn't know my situation and I said, "Lord, have I done anything that can count for anything?" I was feeling sorry for myself because I had been picked on and I said, "Lord, is there anything at all I have done in this ministry that counts for anything?" I think we have all been there if we are being honest with ourselves.

Well, that week a friend of mine that worked at Microsoft was looking on my web page and he said to me, "Alberta, do you know there's a book on your web page? A whole chapter in the book is about you being in Gloria Gillespie's church." Long story short, he was reminding me that Gloria had put a chapter about me in <u>Arise and Shine</u>, and I didn't even know at that time. I said, "No." He said, "It's on your web page. You should have known." He said, "Read this chapter, 'Dancing With Jesus'." I thought, "Well, what is that?" Gloria had written that book, and I didn't know that there was a chapter in there about when I ministered there. So, I read this chapter, "Dancing With Jesus," and I cried. I said, "Lord, where have I been that I would forget?" A lot of times we minister, and we forget the good things and only concentrate sometimes on the negative.

This chapter is about a little four-year-old girl, Pastor Gillespie's granddaughter. She had come to one of my meetings. I had held a three-day meeting there, and it was a powerful, powerful meeting. This little girl comes over and she jumps on her grandma's lap. Gloria was seated right by me. Then she says to me and Gloria, "Grandma, can't you see all the angels here? Can't you see when they sing songs about the Lord, those angels are clapping? Can't you see them grandma? How beautiful they are?" Gloria and I couldn't see them, but she could. Then she says something that was so surprising and shocking. She says, "Grandma, Alberta, can't you see Jesus is here? He's down there. He's praying for that woman down there. He's here." Gloria and I said, "Well, that's nice, sweetheart, that Jesus is here." but she actually saw Jesus.

I asked Gloria about this, and Gloria told me that she always danced with Jesus. Gloria would often find her in the kitchen, and she'd be dancing. "Who are you dancing with?" Gloria would ask. "I'm dancing with Jesus she would reply, "Can't you see him, Grandma?" Gloria said they would go in a store somewhere and right away her little granddaughter, only four years old, would be inviting people to church in the store. "Hey, hey mister, will you come to my church?" she would ask. They couldn't resist, so they would go to her church.

This was a little girl who kept telling her grandma, "I see Jesus. He's here. I'm dancing with him, Grandma." So, after a beautiful, wonderful meeting I left there and two days later you know what happened? I got a phone call, and it was Gloria who said, "Alberta, Macys dead." That was the little four-year-old granddaughter. I said,

"Gloria, what?" She said, "Yeah, she uh... drowned in the pool. She had a heart condition they didn't know she had, and she drowned in the pool." It was so hard, you know, to accept that Macy had now left us. Gloria told me, "We ran to the hospital and when we got there, she was alive for just a little bit." Gloria said, "Alberta, I saw Jesus literally come to her bed and pick her up and walk out with her. Jesus came." Now, folks, I don't know about you, but I know He's that real. Jesus can be anywhere He wants to be. He, Gloria said, carried that little girl off to heaven. What a sight to behold. She saw her little granddaughter carried away. Jesus Himself came and got her.

You might be thinking, "Well, Jesus doesn't do that." He can do anything He wants. If I read the book of John correctly, He created heaven and earth and everything that was and everything that is going to be, Jesus Christ created. So, He can be anywhere and go anywhere He wants, and He was there to carry that little baby away. I know you will never be the same after reading this. There is such peace in that. Some, they're wondering, "Well, is Jesus real and what happened to my little baby that died? Did He carry her away?" This is what I want to declare to you as I close out this book. God is so full of unlimited love and mercy and grace, that every little child that has died is in heaven. Every little aborted baby is in heaven. That's it! Believe me. Little children are being raised in heaven. Jesus never throws anything away. They are in the master's hands.

I knew another little four-year-old girl that was taken

up to heaven and she saw things up there that no four year old would know and came back to tell about it. I talked to her myself so, I know it's a true story. I know another young man that the Lord took to heaven, and they played in a giant waterfall, and the Lord told him things. He was around five, and knew things that no five year old would know. See dear reader, Jesus is real, and He can be wherever He wants to be. He's real and you've got to know that. Maybe you had an abortion, which I don't condemn anybody for, that's between you and God but if you've aborted a baby and you accept Jesus in your heart and in your life, you will see that baby again. He, the Lord, doesn't waste anything. The minute that baby dies from abortion or any other way, it's at once taken into heaven and cared for.

Another time, I was having a meeting in Houston, and I looked toward the front door, and we were really packed out. It was a big church. Suddenly, I thought I saw Jesus and some angels coming through the front door in the spirit. I didn't tell anybody and after the service a man brought his little two kids up, one was nine and the other was ten and he brought them up to the front of the church and said, "Alberta, my kids want to tell you something." I said, "What?" They began to tell me they saw Jesus come in and that He had angels with Him when He came into the service. I've known Him to personally come into different meetings and show up in person.

Some parents out there, they're wondering, "Where did my little baby go? The one that died? Do you know what happened to my little aborted baby?" Well, the minute those little aborted babies die they go right back to Jesus. Remember, the word of God says, "He formed him in His womb", in your womb, the womb of the mother. Jesus said, "He formed them there." He knows those babies, every one of them and when they're aborted, they go right back with Jesus. I have known of women who have actually had an out-of-body experience and went into heaven for a few minutes. One in particular had a little boy come running toward her when she got to heaven and she knew that was the little baby she had aborted. There are a lot of men, you know, they have no say in an abortion. The child is their little baby, but they have no say on if it's killed or not and they wonder where their baby went.

I had them crying in a meeting. They said, "Alberta, we did not know until you told the story in Arise and Shine about little Macy being taken by Jesus at her death. We didn't know where our little babies were" Well, they're in heaven waiting and the Lord is no respecter of persons. When your little child or your little baby dies, the Lord is right there. He takes them right back to glory.

The main thing is knowing Jesus Christ, having Him in your heart and in your life. There is life after death. Jesus is real. I've known Him to show up in person in many places. So, I know that He's alive and He's the Savior of this world. He'll come into your heart, into your life. He'll create a new you. He really will. He'll give you life, and he will give it more abundantly.

When we get to heaven, we're going to know our loved ones when we get there too.

To know Jesus, one can call out to Him with honesty, and He will make Himself real. The process of salvation involves believing in your heart and confessing with your mouth that Jesus is Lord, as stated in Romans 10:10;

10 For with the heart man believeth unto righteousness; and with the mouth confession is made unto salvation.

So, the thing to do is to repent of your sins, ask Jesus into your heart, into your life. He'll come in, and it's not complicated. It's very easy. Just pray this prayer. Say, "Lord Jesus, I believe You died on the cross and rose again on the third day. Forgive me of my sins. Come into my heart and into my life and be Lord of my life." And then be honest with Him.

.

BIOGRAPHY

Apostle Alberta has been in the ministry for many years. She believes in living a Spirit-filled life, and is used by the Lord in the gifts of the Holy Spirit to help people live a more abundant life, and uses the battle cry of John 10:10 to war against the enemy and bring healing, hope and salvation to the multitudes - "The thief does not come except to steal, and to kill, and to destroy. I have come that they may have life, and that they may have it more abundantly."

Affectionately called 'The General', to many who know her, Apostle Alberta preaches a victorious Jesus Christ who died on the cross, rose from the dead, completed our salvation and that He is the Lord of all things. She believes that healing is for today, moves in the 5-Fold and with the unlimited power of the Holy Spirit, brings deliverance to those who are oppressed. She has a strong prophetic gift and often releases Words of wisdom and knowledge.

Throughout many decades of ministry, Alberta has been a guest speaker in many churches, Full Gospel Businessmen's Fellowship meetings, ministered at Women's Aglow, and has delivered the Word and brought signs and wonders to many home meetings in various states. She has appeared on the Daystar Television Network and Trinity Broadcasting Network(TBN) countless times in Washington, Arizona as well as Dallas and Houston, TX. Early in Alberta's ministry she appeared on the 700 Club.